J. Lynett Gillette

DINOSAUR GHOSTS
◆ THE MYSTERY OF COELOPHYSIS ◆

Pictures by **Douglas Henderson**

Dial Books for Young Readers *New York*

To Ned and Margaret —J.L.G.

◆◆◆◆◆

Acknowledgments

Appreciation and special thank you's are given to Alex Downs, Howard Hutchison,
Jean-Michel Galloy, Hilde Schwartz, Ned and Margaret Colbert, Dave and Jennifer Gillette,
the staff at the Ghost Ranch Conference Center, and my editor, Cindy Kane,
for much help and encouragement in the preparation of this book. —J.L.G.

Published by Dial Books for Young Readers
A Division of Penguin Books USA Inc.
375 Hudson Street • New York, New York 10014

Printed in Hong Kong
First Edition
3 5 7 9 10 8 6 4

Library of Congress Cataloging in Publication Data
Gillette, J. Lynett
Dinosaur ghosts : the mystery of Coelophysis / by J. Lynett Gillette;
pictures by Douglas Henderson.—1st ed.
p.   cm.
ISBN 0-8037-1721-0.—ISBN 0-8037-1722-9 (lib.)
1. Coelophysis—Juvenile literature. [1. Coelophysis. 2. Dinosaurs. 3. Paleontology.]
I. Henderson, Douglas, ill. II. Title.
QE862.S3G58 1997   567.9'7—dc20   94-46818   CIP   AC

The full-color paintings are rendered in pastels, while art on back cover and page 14 is drawn in pen and ink.

Photo credits:
Photographs are © Ruth Hall Museum of Paleontology unless otherwise specified.
All appear by permission: Photos of Ghost Ranch p. 3, *Coelophysis* leg bone p. 7, *Coelophysis* skeleton p. 13 by Laurence P. Byers;
photos of AMNH field crew p. 4, Colbert team p. 6, Colbert's telegram p. 7, AMNH crew p. 8 © E. H. Colbert;
photo of Charles Camp's field crew p. 5 © Sam Welles; photo of Downs and Gillette p. 13 by Marshal Hill;
photo of *Coelophysis* sculpture p. 31: sculpture by Dave Thomas, photo by Joan Davidge.

The red and green hills of Ghost Ranch

THERE IS A SAYING that the place called Ghost Ranch in New Mexico got its name because each night after dark, its fossils come out of the ground to play.

No one has really seen this happen, of course. But if there *were* such a thing as a dinosaur ghost, the red and green hills of this beautiful ranch would be filled with them. Hundreds of *Coelophysis* (SEEL-oh-FIE-sis) dinosaurs perished together here, in a tangle of necks, tails, arms, and legs. And for years scientists have been haunted by the question: Why did so many little dinosaurs die at Ghost Ranch?

To begin to answer that question, we must go back in time to the summer of 1947, when a scientist made a spectacular find.

A Big Find of Small Dinosaurs

EDWIN COLBERT listened carefully to his field assistant's excited report. Bones—lots of very small ones—lay on a hillside in a nearby canyon!

Ned Colbert was a paleontologist (a scientist who studies prehistoric life) from the American Museum of Natural History in New York City. His plan was to spend that summer of 1947 collecting fossils in Arizona. On his way to Arizona, Colbert had stopped to take a look around Ghost Ranch north of Albuquerque, New Mexico. He knew fossils had been collected there years earlier by several other paleontologists.

Edwin Colbert, *center*, and the American Museum of Natural History's field crew at Ghost Ranch

Charles Camp's field crew from the University of California at Berkeley, 1933

Some of the earlier fossils had been found by a professor named Charles Camp. Most of the bones Camp discovered were from animals that had lived during the Triassic period of the earth's history, which lasted from 245 to 208 million years ago. Every fossil discovery was faithfully recorded in Camp's field diary. (In this same diary, Camp had mentioned his fantasy of the fossils coming out to dance at night.)

None of Camp's fossils had ever been found in the canyons of Ghost Ranch. But Ned Colbert had an open mind about the canyons. Whenever people asked him his secret for finding fossils, he answered, "Fossils are where you find them, and you find them in the darndest places." He decided to investigate his assistant's report.

The Colbert team digs to uncover more and more bones.

Colbert and his two helpers followed a trail of bone uphill. When the trail ended, the men dug into the hill—and dinosaur skeletons began appearing. The team had found *Coelophysis,* a meat-eating dinosaur about the size of a dog.

Colbert wasn't the first to find this little dinosaur. Back in the 1880's, paleontologist Edward D. Cope hired a fossil collector to find bones for him in northern New Mexico. Traveling with a sure-footed burro, this fossil hunter discovered bits of backbones, a hipbone, a shoulder bone, and the end of a leg bone of a small reptile.

Coelophysis leg bone; a house key helps to show its size.

Cope said the fragile bones were those of a new small dinosaur. He named it *Coelophysis,* "hollow form," to suggest its hollow bones. The discovery didn't receive much publicity. Cope turned to other projects, and few people thought about this little dinosaur for nearly seventy years.

But in the summer of 1947 Colbert's team began finding dozens and dozens of *Coelophysis* skeletons, buried in 225 million-year-old rocks from near the end of the Triassic period. There were so many skeletons that

Colbert had to send a telegram back to the American Museum to ask for more help with the excavation.

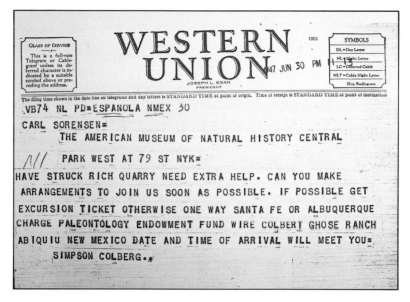

Colbert's telegram to the American Museum of Natural History asking for more help

This was a great find. Most dinosaurs are known from just a few specimens. Up until that time, the most familiar small dinosaurs were two chicken-sized *Compsognathus* skeletons. In a few days *The New York Times* announced the discovery of *Coelophysis* on its front page. A photographer from *Life* magazine visited the site. *Coelophysis* became the best-known small dinosaur ever discovered.

But why were all these dinosaurs buried in one place? Colbert wasn't sure. With Ghost Ranch's permission, he cut blocks of rock with the bones still inside to take to New York for study.

Because the dinosaurs were packed so tightly together, the blocks were made extra large to avoid cutting through a skeleton. Each block weighed a ton or more. Blocks of bone were shared with other museums and universities around the United States for examination, and new paleontologists joined the study of *Coelophysis*.

The American Museum's field crew plasters *Coelophysis* bones to prepare them for travel.

Bone Studies

OVER THE NEXT FIFTY YEARS a more complete picture of *Coelophysis* emerged. Paleontologists saw that the living animal had been a carnivore, or meat eater. Its teeth were sharp along the edges, much like a steak knife—perfect for slicing. Short front legs with sharp claws helped to hold the dinosaur's prey, but the long, flexible neck and strong jaws did most of the work.

They were lively, graceful animals, built for speed. The long, slender leg bones allowed *Coelophysis* to run upright, much like an African secretary bird does today. And much like a bird, *Coelophysis* had fragile, thin bones. If a technician working on *Coelophysis* sneezed, small bone fragments would fly into the air. Inside the whole length of each thin leg and arm bone was a very wide space called the marrow cavity, where red blood cells were made. Active animals need plenty of red blood cells to carry oxygen.

Scientists think *Coelophysis* may have lived in large family groups, possibly in herds. We know that the young stayed with the adults for several years because all ages except embryos in eggs and newborn hatchlings have been found at Ghost Ranch. They probably ate other reptiles—such as young phytosaurs, which resembled alligators—plus fish, crayfish, clams, and in some cases even their own kind. Two skeletons of *Coelophysis* have their last meal still in the belly: small bones of a young *Coelophysis*. Some reptiles today still have this habit of cannibalism.

Coelophysis of all ages hunted for prey along the edges of rivers and lakes.

Unlike many other Triassic reptiles, *Coelophysis* dinosaurs had no armor to shield them from predators. Instead, speed and agility gave an advantage to *Coelophysis* when facing a hungry armored phytosaur. Large eyes also may have helped *Coelophysis* find prey, even in the dim light of early morning and evening when more sluggish reptiles might be napping.

What Happened Here?

AFTER STUDYING THE *Coelophysis* bones to learn what these dinosaurs were like when they were alive, the scientists turned their attention to the positions of the bones in the ground. The arrangement of the bones might give some clues to the mystery of what happened to all these dinosaurs. Why and how did they die?

Many nearly complete skeletons were found with almost all their bones still joined together. These skeletons lay flat on their sides with their heads, tails, hands, and feet all at about the same level. When these dinosaurs died, strong muscles in their necks tightened and pulled the neck and head back in a curve toward the tail.

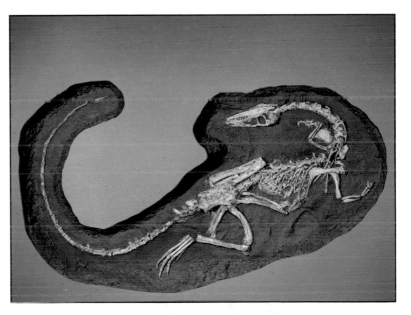

A nearly complete *Coelophysis* skeleton, showing curving and twisting of the neck after death. In the belly are bones of a young *Coelophysis*.

Alex Downs, *right,* and J. Lynett Gillette study the position of the bones.

In a different arrangement, some skeletons had missing bones and also were separated. Necks were no longer joined to bodies, tails were not attached to hips, ribs did not touch backbones. These bones had no unusual breaks or tooth marks, so we know the skeletons weren't scattered by predators.

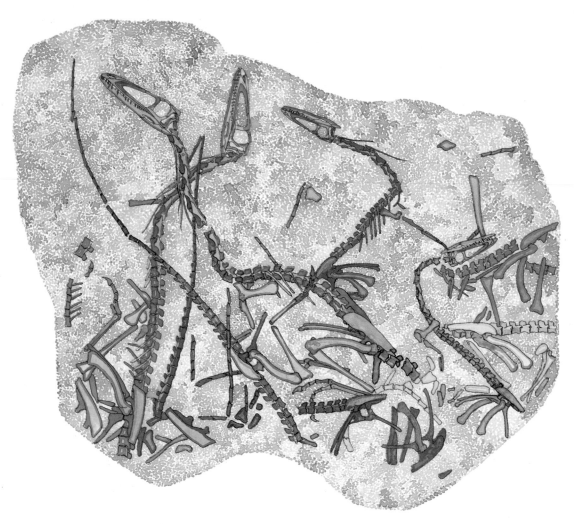

Clusters of skeletons with separated bones

Smaller animals living in the ancient river included fish, freshwater clams, swimming reptiles, and crayfish.

All the skeletons—the nearly complete ones, stretched out on their sides, and the separated ones—lay close together. Some were even piled on top of one another. Other animals were discovered with the *Coelophysis* skeletons: a few fish, phytosaurs, small members of the crocodile family, and a very small lizard. The place where all these animals were buried is about thirty feet long and at least thirty feet wide. Around the bones are red rocks made of mud once carried by an ancient river.

Looking closely at the skeletons, paleontologists could see that none of the bones of any of the dinosaurs or the other animals seemed to be cracked from drying a long time in the sun. After considering this fact and all the other clues from the bones, the scientists have suggested a number of possible scenes that might explain the *Coelophysis* burial ground at Ghost Ranch. We can test these scientific suggestions, or hypotheses, by comparing them with the evidence found in the bones and the rocks around them.

Stuck in the Mud?

A *Coelophysis* STEPS TO the river's edge, coming to feed on several fish that are splashing in a pool of water. The dinosaur's feet sink deep in the dark, sticky earth. Other dinosaurs gather, also attracted by the splashing fish, but they too are caught in the treacherous ground. No matter how hard they struggle, they are all trapped, young and old alike.

The La Brea tar pits in California were once the site of scenes like this one. Thousands of animals were trapped there in sticky pools of black tar during the Ice Ages. Did a similar thing happen at Ghost Ranch?

Probably not. If the dinosaurs *had* been trapped in mud, as they struggled their heavier legs would be buried more deeply than their arms and heads, and their bodies would be upright. (This is what scientists believe happened to a Triassic dinosaur from Europe called *Plateosaurus* that died after being trapped in mud.) Since so many *Coelophysis* were found lying on their sides, most likely they didn't die this way.

Volcanic Violence?

THE LITTLE DINOSAURS ARE surprised by an erupting volcano as they gather at a river's edge to eat. They cannot breathe in the hot, swiftly moving clouds of ash and sulfurous gases. In great panic they fall down as they scramble to escape. Soon they are buried by mud slides flowing down the river valley and by ash falling from the sky.

Many of the earth's great catastrophes have been caused by erupting volcanoes. When Mount St. Helens in Washington state blew its top in 1980, animals that couldn't run or burrow into the earth were killed by the heat, ash, and poisonous gases.

Does the scene at Ghost Ranch fit this picture? It doesn't seem likely to the geologists who have begun to study the rocks in which the *Coelophysis* skeletons are buried. If there were even traces of volcanic ash, under the microscope the rocks would have a few tiny smashed bubbles of the mineral silica. This silica would be present in the fiery blobs of ash shot into the sky. But no collapsed silica bubbles have been found yet in the rocks.

Asteroids From Outer Space?

THE SUN ISN'T AS BRIGHT as usual, because high gray dust clouds shield the earth. The animals that the *Coelophysis* dinosaurs usually eat are becoming hard to find. The dinosaurs have become very thin; their scales are dull. Their tails—normally carried high—are drooping. Weak and exhausted, the dinosaurs fall, one by one, and do not get up.

Scientists Walter and Luis Alvarez of the University of California have suggested a reason why dinosaurs became extinct around 65 million years ago. The Alvarezes said that maybe a huge asteroid falling out of orbit from outer space struck the earth. The collision would have sent great clouds of dust into the air that blocked sunlight and cooled the earth. A cooler earth couldn't support the same kinds of plants and animals. Many species that needed warm temperatures would die.

Not all paleontologists accept this reason for the extinction of dinosaurs, but it is an attractive one. A small amount of a rare element—iridium—has been found in many 65 million-year-old rocks. Asteroids often have more iridium than earth rocks, so an asteroid may indeed have brought this element to earth. Could an earlier asteroid, 225 million years ago, have caused climatic changes that killed *Coelophysis*?

The facts don't fit this picture at Ghost Ranch. The dinosaurs aren't scattered over a large area, as they would be if they collapsed, one by one, from hunger. And so far no one has found unusual amounts of iridium in the rocks. Asteroid extinctions don't seem to agree with what we have learned about *Coelophysis*.

Poisoned Water?

A GROUP OF *Coelophysis* gathers at a spring-fed pool of water along the river's edge. Balancing on their small front legs, they crouch down and drink, unaware that the water is poisoned. In a short time, one by one, they fall to the ground and die. Others come the next day, and the same thing happens again.

Do we find any poisons in the bones or the rocks around the dinosaur "graveyard" at Ghost Ranch? If the dinosaurs were killed this way, some poisons might remain, even after millions of years.

Geologists have tested the rocks and they did find a poison, arsenic, in both the rocks and the bones! But there are two problems with this theory.

First, we can't know exactly *when* the arsenic got into the bones and rocks. Just because arsenic is in the bones now doesn't mean that it was there when the dinosaurs died. The arsenic might have seeped in, carried by underground water, many years later.

And there's another idea to consider. Phytosaurs and fish were found with the dinosaurs. Could they have survived in a poisoned water hole? Poison that would kill dinosaurs would probably make the water unfit for other animals too—especially ones that had to live *in* the water. For this reason arsenic doesn't seem to fit what we know either.

A Fearsome Flood?

A GROUP OF *Coelophysis* dinosaurs sleep in their resting area away from the riverbank under tall evergreen trees. It has been raining for days. This night the rising water spills over the top of the river channel and rushes down a wide valley. *Coelophysis* groups from many areas wake and begin to run, but the water is too fast. They are caught up and drowned by the churning flood. A few dinosaurs who run up the valley, instead of down, are saved.

Soon the rain clouds pass, and the river returns to its old channel. Down the valley rest the bodies of hundreds of dinosaurs, with a few phytosaurs, fish, and other reptiles. They are wrapped together, necks over tails, one on top of the other.

The rains aren't finished yet. Another tropical storm begins, and the river floods again. New mud and water flow into the old riverbed and cover the dinosaurs before other predators arrive.

The tangled positions and good condition of the skeletons (no cracks from the sun, no tooth marks from predators) might well have been caused by a flood. After the dinosaurs drowned, they could have been thrown together by a rush of floodwater and mud and buried quickly.

But if this is true, how do we explain those dinosaur skeletons that were found on their sides with the necks curved toward the tails? This position happens only if a dead animal, such as a cow lying in a field, is undisturbed long enough for its muscles and ligaments to shrink. Why were these dinosaurs arranged differently than the rest? Even the suggestion of a flood doesn't fit all the clues.

Water Worries?

THE SUN HAS BURNED in a cloudless sky for days and days. Ponds, streams, and lakes are drying up. Plants are dying. Plant eaters are starving. Crayfish are burrowing deep into mud to wait for wetter days. Fish are trapped by the hundreds in ever smaller puddles. *Coelophysis* gather to scoop up the helpless fish, but even more than meat, the dinosaurs need water.

As more fish are trapped, more *Coelophysis* of all ages come to eat. But the feeding activity doesn't last. The dinosaurs are weak with hunger and thirst, and there isn't enough food or drink to satisfy everyone. Hundreds die as they crowd around the last of the puddles.

When paleontologists began looking at the rocks around the bones of these dinosaurs, they sometimes found mud cracks, suggesting that some of the animals died on sun-baked mud. The skeletons with the curved necks were arranged like any animal who dries out in the hot sun after death.

Most of the fish bones were underneath the dinosaurs, as if they had attracted the little hunters to the site. And the scientists found many places where crayfish had burrowed into the mud.

But the drought picture does not tell the whole story. We already know that the dinosaurs' bones were not cracked by drying a long time in the sun. What if they spent only a short time—just a few days—in the sun?

The real picture may be a combination of two suggestions—a drought *and* a flood.

Too Little Water—
Then Too Much

MANY OF THE LITTLE dinosaurs die at the end of a dry season when the earth is baked and the water holes are dry. One day the *Coelophysis* that are still alive discover a few sickly fish swimming slowly back and forth in a puddle at the bottom of the riverbed. Other fish bodies have already sunk into the mud. When a sudden rainstorm breaks the drought, a surge of water and thick mud flows swiftly over the riverbanks and down the valley. *Coelophysis* and other predators are trapped in the flood and drown.

When the waters dry up, they leave behind both the dinosaurs that had died a few days earlier in the drought and the newly drowned dinosaurs. Some are dropped in tangles; some lie alone, stretched out on the mud. The ones that lie in puddles begin to separate. Those outside the puddles begin to dry and shrink. Soon fresh rains bring more mud. The dinosaurs are buried completely in a few days, and they stay that way for millions of years. They are not uncovered until erosion in a canyon removes their blanket of rock in 1947.

This is our best idea for what happened to *Coelophysis* on those fateful days over two hundred million years ago. We can't say for sure that it is the right answer—but it's the explanation that fits most of the clues Ned Colbert and other scientists have discovered so far.

Coelophysis sculpture in today's Ghost Ranch landscape

Could more information turn up that might point us toward a whole new scene? Of course, since the site is still being studied. Scientists are always ready to change their ideas to fit what they learn. New discoveries about the fossils and rocks at Ghost Ranch can still be made by anyone with the patience to study them—and the luck to find them "in the darndest places."

Index and Pronunciation Guide

Boldface page numbers refer to illustrations